WALT DISNEY

By Elizabeth Dana Jaffe

Please visit our web site at: www.worldalmanaclibrary.com
For a free color catalog describing World Almanac® Library's list of high-quality books
and multimedia programs, call 1-800-848-2928 (USA) or 1-800-461-9120 (Canada).
World Almanac® Library's Fax: (414) 332-3567.

Library of Congress Cataloging-in-Publication Data

Jaffe, Elizabeth Dana.
    Walt Disney / by Elizabeth Dana Jaffe.
       p. cm. — (Trailblazers of the modern world)
    Includes bibliographical references and index.
    Summary: A biography of the man who began his career as an animator and became the creator of Mickey Mouse and Disneyland, and the founder of Disney Studios.
    ISBN 0-8368-5062-9 (lib. bdg.)
    ISBN 0-8368-5222-2 (softcover)
    1. Disney, Walt, 1901-1966—Juvenile literature. 2. Animators—United States—Biography—Juvenile literature.
    [1. Disney, Walt, 1901-1966. 2. Motion pictures—Biography.] I. Title. II. Series.
NC1766.U52J34   2001
791.43'092—dc21
    [B]   2001034180

Updated and reprinted in 2005
This North American edition first published in 2001 by
World Almanac® Library
330 West Olive Street, Suite 100
Milwaukee, WI 53212 USA

This U.S. edition © 2001 by World Almanac® Library.

An Editorial Directions book
Editor: Lucia Raatma
Designer and page production: Ox and Company
Photo researcher: Dawn Friedman
Indexer: Timothy Griffin
Proofreader: Neal Durando
World Almanac® Library art direction: Karen Knutson
World Almanac® Library editor: Jacqueline Laks Gorman
World Almanac® Library production: Susan Ashley and Jessica L. Yanke

Photo credits: AP/Wide World Photos, cover; Hulton/Archive, 4, 5, 7; Corbis/Minnesota Historical Society, 9 top; Corbis/Detroit Photo Company, 9 bottom; Corbis/Lewis W. Hine, 10; Hulton/Archive, 12; Corbis/Bettmann, 13 top; AP/Wide World Photos, 13 bottom; Corbis/Bettmann, 14; AP/Wide World Photos, 16; Hulton/Archive, 17; Corbis/Bettmann, 18; Hulton/Archive, 19, 22, 23; Corbis/Hulton-Deutsch Collection, 24; Hulton/Archive, 25, 26 top; AP/Wide World Photos, 26 bottom; Corbis/Bettmann, 27 top; Hulton/Archive, 27 bottom; Corbis/Bettmann, 28 top; AP/Wide World Photos, 28 bottom, 29; Corbis/Paul Almasy, 31; Hulton/Archive, 32; AP/Wide World Photos, 33; Hulton/Archive/Gene Lester, 34; AP/Wide World Photos, 35, 36; Corbis/Bettmann, 37; AP/Wide World Photos, 39 top; Corbis, 39 bottom; Hulton/Archive/Frank Capri, Saga, 40 top; Hulton/Archive, 40 bottom, 41 top; AP/Wide World Photos/Randi Lynn Beach, 41 bottom; AP/Wide World Photos/Gail Oskin, 42 left; Hulton/Archive, 42 right; Corbis/Kelly-Mooney Photography, 43.

All rights reserved. No part of this book may be reproduced, stored in a retrieval system, or transmitted in any form or by any means, electronic, mechanical, photocopying, recording, or otherwise without the prior written permission of the copyright holder.

Printed in the United States of America

3 4 5 6 7 8 9 09 08 07 06 05

TABLE of CONTENTS

CHAPTER 1	A MAGICAL MAN	4
CHAPTER 2	YOUNG WALT'S IMAGINATION	7
CHAPTER 3	BECOMING AN ARTIST	12
CHAPTER 4	MAKING HISTORY	18
CHAPTER 5	AT HOME AND AT THE STUDIO	24
CHAPTER 6	CREATING A KINGDOM	31
CHAPTER 7	LEAVING A LEGACY	38
	TIMELINE	44
	GLOSSARY	45
	TO FIND OUT MORE	46
	INDEX	47

CHAPTER 1
A MAGICAL MAN

Walt Disney found success by entertaining his audiences.

Walt Disney is one of the most famous names in today's world. Millions of people visit Disneyland and Walt Disney World each year, while millions more watch movies and TV shows produced by the Disney studio. Around the world, the Disney characters of Mickey Mouse, Goofy, and Donald Duck adorn T-shirts and sweatshirts, watches, and hats. However, the remarkable success that we see surrounding Disney did not come easily. Walt Disney had a vision for entertaining the world, but it took years of hard work and perseverance for his vision to become a reality. Behind all the characters, products, and films is the life of an ordinary man—but a man of great imagination and determination.

MORE THAN MICKEY MOUSE

The great big ears of Mickey Mouse are known throughout the United States and everywhere else, but Walt Disney did more than create this friendly character. He made great strides in **animation**, introduced sound to cartoons, and gave us the first full-length animated feature film.

Disney suffered many failures, but in the end, he won numerous **Academy Awards** and was honored with the Presidential Medal of Freedom, the highest honor a U.S. citizen can receive. He took great risks in his business, but he ultimately made history.

HARD WORK AND MORE HARD WORK

Over the years, Disney put in countless hours as an artist and as the head of a film studio too. He was a driven man who expected a lot from himself—and from everyone around him. Many of his workers loved Disney and remained forever loyal to him, while others resented the long hours and low pay so much that personnel problems at the studio often plagued Disney's life.

Mickey and Minnie Mouse are two of Disney's most famous creations.

Through it all, Walt Disney strove for excellence. He put his heart into all his creations, and he inspired others as well. Even when his ideas seemed impossible, Disney was determined to see his projects through to the end. Many people thought Disney's big dreams were crazy. However, Walt Disney was strengthened by the support of his brother Roy and the love of his wife and daughters. Disney always believed in himself, and that confidence resulted in the creation of an entertainment empire.

YOUNG WALT'S IMAGINATION

CHAPTER 2

Walter Elias Disney was born in Chicago, Illinois, on December 5, 1901. His parents, Elias and Flora, already had three sons—Herbert, Raymond, and Roy. Two years later, they added a daughter, Ruth, to their family.

As Elias began to worry about big-city life, he decided to move his family from Chicago to a 45-acre (18-hectare) farm outside Marceline, Missouri. The farm had cows, pigs, chickens, and ducks, and behind the house was a huge apple orchard.

Walt Disney was born in Chicago in 1901.

LIFE ON THE FARM

Elias Disney worked hard and expected everyone in his family to do the same. The Disney children were given chores to do every day, and the older boys, who were then teenagers, did the hardest labor. Young Walt was in charge of the animals, a job that he loved. Walt named them all and considered a few to be his best friends. Flora appreciated her son's attachment to the animals. Little did she know that these animals would someday inspire Walt to create his wonderful characters.

Remembering Marceline

As a child, Walt Disney loved to draw and to use his imagination. When he looked at farm animals, he saw characters, and when he looked at blank paper, he saw the beginnings of a wonderful cartoon or story. Later in life, he remembered:

More things of importance happened to me in Marceline than have happened since—or are likely to happen in the future.

AN ARTISTIC MIND

Walt sketched animals on any paper he could find—usually bits of wrapping paper or toilet paper. One day, at age seven, Walt found a barrel of fresh tar. He and Ruth used the black, sticky substance to draw on the side of their house, never realizing that the tar would dry. Later, Walt tried to rub the drawings off the side of the house, but—to his dismay—they wouldn't budge. Those pictures were there to stay.

In another creative venture, young Walt once staged a circus in his backyard. With a couple of unruly cats and a tent made of burlap sacks, Walt's show was not much of a success. Nevertheless, his creative mind kept on churning.

Roy recognized how special his brother was, and he encouraged Walt's creativity. Whenever he could, he bought sketchpads or new toys for Walt. The older boy seemed to enjoy making Walt happy, and this brotherly devotion continued for the rest of their lives.

HARD TIMES

Keeping the farm running meant working long hours in the fields. While Roy, Walt, and Ruth were in school, Elias insisted that Herbert and Raymond help him—from sunrise to sunset every day. By 1908, however, the two young men were tired of working for their demanding father, and one night they ran away from home. Elias was bitterly disappointed in his sons and could not keep up with the demands of the farm without them. Two years later,

the situation got even worse when Elias contracted **typhoid fever**, a serious illness. Although his health eventually improved, Elias would always be weak thereafter. The Disneys knew it was time to sell the farm.

The Disneys worked a Missouri farm similar to this one.

ON TO KANSAS CITY

After the farm was sold, Elias moved his family to Kansas City, Missouri, and invested all their money in a paper route for the Kansas City Star. Elias was too weak to deliver the papers, but he expected Walt and Roy to do the job.

It was not an easy task. At 3:30 each morning, Elias shook Walt and Roy awake. For the next two hours, they

After selling their farm, the Disneys moved to Kansas City, Missouri.

and the other boys Elias hired would deliver heavy stacks of newspapers to two thousand customers. Then, after Walt's morning deliveries, he had to go to school. Walt often fell asleep in class, but then he had his afternoon newspaper deliveries to make after school.

Roy and Walt watched the other boys getting paid $3 a week to deliver papers and wondered why they got nothing. Elias explained that he provided them with food, clothing, and shelter, and that was more than enough. Roy, who was then seventeen, began to understand why his two older brothers had left home. It was not long before he left too, taking a job as a bank teller in Kansas City.

Walt was sorry to see Roy go, but he just continued working as best he could. In fact, he went behind Elias's back and ordered fifty more papers to sell. With the extra money, Walt bought candy and drawing paper. Life wasn't easy, but Walt made the best of it.

> ### Understanding His Father
>
> Elias Disney may have been a difficult man, but Walt had great respect for him. Later in life, he explained it this way:
>
> *I don't want anyone to think my father was a tyrant, but he did have a terrible temper, and he was always trying to make you do things for which you weren't suitable.*

opposite: Roy and Walt Disney delivered newspapers much in the way these boys did.

CHAPTER 3
BECOMING AN ARTIST

Walt Disney's creative spirit showed not only in his drawings but also in his love of the stage. He enjoyed performing for his classmates and friends. He and his friends also went to see shows at movie theaters and **vaudeville** houses. They especially loved watching Charlie Chaplin, a famous silent film star at that time.

CHICAGO AND BEYOND

After a few years, Elias sold the newspaper route and moved the family back to Chicago. By this time, Walt was sixteen years old. While still in high school, he took some art courses at the Art Institute of Chicago and served as art editor for the school newspaper.

Charlie Chaplin

Charlie Chaplin was an actor, director, and producer during the silent film era (and later as well). He became best known for a character called the Little Tramp, who carried a cane and wore a derby hat, baggy trousers, and oversized shoes. Skipping across the screen in a comical bow-legged walk, he won the hearts of movie-going audiences.

In that role, he developed "The Tiny Voice," a cartoon strip about World War I (1914–1918).

The United States had entered the war in 1917. Walt wanted to join the army, but he was too young. However, when he found out that the Red Cross Ambulance Unit took volunteers who were seventeen, Walt lied about his age and enlisted. The war ended on November 11, 1918, but Walt was still sent to France to help the wounded soldiers. There he used his artistic skills for decorating the ambulances and making souvenirs for soldiers to take back home.

Disney took courses at the Art Institute of Chicago.

The Red Cross Ambulance Unit in World War I

HIS TURN TO LEAVE

When Walt arrived back in Chicago in late 1919, he told his father he wanted to be an artist. Elias thought this was a foolish idea and did not want a son who drew pictures for a living. At that point, Walt saw no reason to remain in Chicago with his disapproving father. He decided to join Roy in Kansas City.

Walt Disney's first job in Kansas City was as an **apprentice** at Pesmen-Rubin Commercial Art Studio, a company that produced artwork for other companies' advertisements. Disney met a fellow apprentice there named Ub Iwerks, and they became fast friends. Iwerks was serious, quiet, and extremely shy—and also very talented.

Disney at his drawing table

ON THEIR OWN

After Christmas that year, the company didn't have enough work for Disney and Iwerks, so they were fired. Disney suggested that they start their own advertising business, and Iwerks agreed. They named their studio Iwerks-Disney, and for a month, things went well.

Meanwhile, Disney applied for a job at the Kansas City Film Ad Company. Disney hoped that if he got the job, the company would also hire Iwerks. Unfortunately, after the company employed Disney, it didn't need another artist. Iwerks still encouraged Disney to take the job while he ran Iwerks-Disney. Eventually, Iwerks-Disney went out of business, but the Kansas City Film Ad Company hired Iwerks shortly thereafter.

CARTOON ANIMATION

The Kansas City Film Ad Company made one-minute animated ads that were shown in movie theaters. Disney found animation exciting, but he became frustrated with the process used by the company. Its way of filming cut-out doll figures resulted in awkward, jerky films. Disney and Iwerks learned of a way to speed up and smooth out animation with a process that involved filming a series of paintings drawn on sheets of material called **celluloid.**

LAUGH-O-GRAMS

Using this new process and a borrowed camera, Disney made short, funny cartoons called Laugh-O-Grams. He sold the cartoons to a theater where they were shown before the movies started. Soon the theater paid Disney to make more. Laugh-O-Grams became so successful that Disney was able to leave the Kansas City Film Ad Company and open up his own business—Laugh-O-Gram Films. Walt hired young **animators** who wanted to learn how to draw cartoons and who were willing to work for free. Because each second of screen time took twenty-four drawings, more than fourteen thousand drawings were needed for each ten-minute film. Clearly, Disney needed a lot of help—and the best help possible—so he hired his old friend Ub Iwerks.

Meanwhile, Disney continued to experiment with a cartoon series, called *Alice's Wonderland*, that combined live action with animation. He filmed a child actress and made it look as though she was interacting with cartoon characters on film.

Disney (left) and Ub Iwerks (next to him) on the set for a film

Unfortunately, Disney did not receive all the money he was promised because the people who had hired him to provide cartoons went out of business. Disney was left with nothing but debts. Eventually, he also went out of business and had to let all of his employees go. Soon, twenty-one-year-old Disney had to declare **bankruptcy**.

> ### Failure
>
> It would have been easy for young Walt Disney to give up his dreams. At twenty-one, he had already seen both Iwerks-Disney and Laugh-O-Gram Films fail. However, Disney kept a positive attitude and once said: "I think it's important to have a good hard failure when you're young."

HIS NEXT MOVE

In July 1923, Walt Disney wanted to move to either New York or California, and he decided on the latter. At the time his brother Roy was sick with **tuberculosis** in a hospital in Los Angeles. Disney packed his last few possessions and headed to Hollywood. There he would be closer to his brother—and closer to the action of moviemaking.

Hollywood was an appealing place for young Walt Disney.

17

CHAPTER 4

MAKING HISTORY

When Disney first arrived in Hollywood, he wanted to direct **live-action films** rather than create cartoons. However, he lacked the necessary experience to get a job. During the 1920s, many people hoped to find work in Hollywood. Silent films were popular, and movie stars were very glamorous—and well paid.

So Disney began thinking about animation again. He remembered a woman named Margaret Winkler, a cartoon **distributor** in New York who had once expressed interest in *Alice's Wonderland*. He sent her one episode, and soon she wanted the whole Alice series.

Roy, who always remained loyal to his brother, filming Walt in Hawaii

BROTHERS AND PARTNERS

Hoping that the Alice cartoons would mean real success, Disney convinced his brother Roy to be his partner. Roy would handle the business end, while Walt would head the creative end. From that point on, Walt and Roy were a team. Initially, they formed the Disney Brothers Studio, and then—at Roy's insistence—they renamed it Walt Disney Studios.

18

The brothers hired twelve staff members, one of whom was Ub Iwerks. Roy Disney proved to be invaluable to his younger brother. He provided Walt with not only emotional support but also financial assistance and advice.

WEDDING BELLS

For a time, the brothers tried to save money by sharing a room and eating as cheaply as they could. However, Roy soon moved out and married Edna Francis, his girlfriend from Kansas City.

In the meantime, Walt had his eye on an employee at the studio. Her name was Lillian Bounds and she was an "ink and paint" girl, meaning she painted animators' drawings onto celluloid. Lilly, as Walt called her, was a very shy young woman from Idaho. Walt found her easy to talk to, and it wasn't long before he proposed. They were married on July 13, 1925.

The Silent Screen

When movies first began, they were made without sound. The words the actors spoke were printed on the screen for audiences to read, while a piano player provided background music in each theater. Among the major stars of the silent film era were Lillian Gish, Buster Keaton, Gloria Swanson, and Rudolph Valentino. This era came to an end when sound was introduced. *The Jazz Singer*, released in 1927, was the first film to have sound, and over the years, more and more advances were made in sound technology.

Disney with his wife, Lilly, in the 1920s

DEALING WITH DISTRIBUTION

Meanwhile, the studio was very busy. The staff had to keep churning out the Alice cartoons, and the pressure was greater than ever. Margaret Winkler had married Charles Mintz, a man who would go on to produce and distribute hundreds of animated films. Sometimes Mintz complained about the quality of the Alice cartoons, and often he threatened not to pay for the work.

In an attempt to please Mintz, Disney worked right through many nights. He was devoted to his work, and he expected his staff to be devoted too. He put a lot of pressure on the artists, settling for nothing less than perfection. What Disney didn't realize was that he was behaving like his father, making demands that others found extremely difficult to satisfy.

OSWALD THE LUCKY RABBIT

Universal Pictures asked Charles Mintz for a new cartoon series based on a rabbit, so he asked Disney to come up with something. Disney and Iwerks created Oswald the Lucky Rabbit, and soon this lovable character became popular all over America.

With Oswald's success, Disney flew to New York to see Mintz, expecting praise and more money. However, unknown to Disney, Mintz had approached many Disney staff members about working for him at a higher salary. So when the two men met, Mintz offered Disney much less money than before, threatening—if Disney turned him down—to take his staff and the Oswald character as well. Disney and Iwerks may have created Oswald, but Mintz owned him.

In the end, Disney refused Mintz's offer. Losing Oswald was a terrible blow to him, but losing his staff was even worse. He had always thought of the studio as a happy family, and he was shocked to learn that many of the artists were dissatisfied. Thus, he felt betrayed and disappointed. The only one who remained loyal to Disney was Ub Iwerks.

CREATING A FAMOUS MOUSE

On the train ride back to California, Disney did a lot of thinking. He realized that he could never work for anyone else again—he needed his freedom. He talked to Lilly about hiring a whole new staff and starting a new series. Through all this talking and thinking, the world's most famous cartoon character was born.

By the time the train reached the Midwest, Disney had drawn a happy mouse wearing a pair of velvet pants with two huge pearl buttons. He first named the character "Mortimer," but Lilly suggested "Mickey." So Mickey Mouse it was.

The Face of Cartoons

Walt Disney made his mark by creating cartoon characters. He once remembered what animation taught him:

In learning the art of storytelling by animation, I have discovered that language has an anatomy. Every spoken word, whether uttered by a living person or by a cartoon character, has its facial grimace, emphasizing the meaning.

A MOUSE THAT TALKS

Once back in Hollywood, Disney and Iwerks worked together on Mickey Mouse. Their first two episodes starring the new character were received fairly well by the audiences, but distributors were not interested. One Universal Pictures representative even said, "Mice?

Who wants mice?" Disney needed something to make Mickey special. Luckily, right about this time, the motion-picture world was undergoing a huge change. *The Jazz Singer*, starring Al Jolson, had just been released—the first film made with sound. No longer did audiences have to read dialogue on the screen. They could hear the actors speak!

Al Jolson in *The Jazz Singer*

This was an exciting development, but some people were hesitant to embrace it. "Talkies," as they were known, would require new sound systems in theaters and new equipment for studios. However, Disney never worried about taking on new challenges. He immediately began working on "Steamboat Willie," a short talking film starring Mickey Mouse. Although other animators had already added background music to their cartoons, Disney planned to be the first to make the voices and music match the action perfectly.

"Steamboat Willie" was introduced on November 18, 1928, in New York City. Everyone fell in love with Mickey Mouse, and Disney got offers from many companies to make Mickey Mouse films for them. But he refused every offer. With Mickey Mouse, Disney wanted creative control and sole ownership.

The *New York Times* praised "Steamboat Willie" as "an ingenious piece of work with a good deal of fun." Mickey Mouse became a star, and the Academy of Motion Picture Arts and Sciences later awarded Disney a special Oscar for creating him. Walt Disney and his mouse had made history.

opposite: Disney with an animated version of Mickey Mouse

CHAPTER 5
AT HOME AND AT THE STUDIO

Though Mickey Mouse was a remarkable success, trouble continued for Walt Disney. He had signed a contract with a New York distributor whom he should never have trusted. The man kept a lot of money he owed Disney and even lured Ub Iwerks away from the Disney studio. Once again, Disney was devastated. Years later, Iwerks asked Disney for a job when he needed one. Disney gave him work, but the two men were never close again.

MOVIES AND THE GREAT DEPRESSION

In 1929, the stock market crash marked the beginning of the **Great Depression**. However, the film business did not suffer because people went to movies to escape from their troubles. With the security of a steady audience, Disney experimented with all the latest technology in his films. He had begun a new series called *Silly Symphonies*, which was enjoying success all over the country. In 1932, one episode in that series, "Flowers and Trees," made history. It was the first cartoon to be made in **Technicolor**, a new way of adding full color to film. It was also the first cartoon ever to win an Academy Award.

Disney and a cameraman studying a live penguin; the film footage was then used by cartoonists working on a new film.

THE DISNEY FAMILY

In 1933, Walt and Lilly Disney celebrated the birth of a daughter, Diane Marie. Three years later, the Disneys adopted Sharon Mae, another baby girl. Walt Disney loved being a father, and he had to try hard not to spoil his daughters. At times, he could be distant with his employees and critical of their work, but he was different with his family, showering his wife and daughters with affection. Diane and Sharon considered him to be their best playmate, and with them, he was silly, kind, and encouraging. Over the years, Disney's family brought him a great deal of support and happiness.

The Multiplane Camera

A special device, called a **multiplane camera**, was invented in the 1930s. This large machine took up most of a room and could shoot through several different layers of celluloid. The camera moved back and forth, creating films with a better sense of movement and a three-dimensional feel. Disney first used the multiplane on a *Silly Symphonies* cartoon called "The Old Mill."

Lilly (center) and daughters Diane (left) and Sharon (right) were a constant source of joy for Walt Disney.

DISNEY'S FOLLY

As much as Walt Disney enjoyed the short cartoons his studio was producing, he decided it was time to make a full-length animated film. Some people thought audiences wouldn't watch a long cartoon, but Disney was convinced he was right.

Snow White and the Seven Dwarfs was to be eighty minutes long and consist of 7,200 feet (2,196 meters) of film. Only ten feet (3 m) could

Disney with some examples of the studio's animation

A scene from *Snow White and the Seven Dwarfs*

be done per week, so even with 750 people working for him, Disney was taking on a monstrous project. When word of his project got out, many people made fun of Disney, referring to the film as "Disney's Folly."

The finished film premiered on December 7, 1937, in New York City, where it received a standing ovation. Critics called *Snow White and the Seven Dwarfs* a masterpiece, and Disney received a special Academy Award for it, the award consisting of one big Oscar and seven little ones—one for each dwarf.

Shirley Temple presented Disney with his Oscars—one big one and seven little ones—for *Snow White and the Seven Dwarfs.*

TRAGEDY AND TRIUMPH

Meanwhile, Disney and his staff continued to create new characters, such as Pluto, Goofy, and the famous Donald Duck. Shortly after the *Snow White* debut, Roy and Walt Disney celebrated by buying a home for their parents in California. Elias, now almost eighty, was amazed by the success of his sons, and he and Flora enjoyed their new lifestyle.

However, in November 1938, a leak from a gas furnace killed Flora. Her death was a terrible blow to the Disney clan, and Elias never really recovered, dying soon after. Roy and Walt were saddened by the loss of their parents, but they never talked about it, instead burying themselves in their work. By 1940, the Disney company had more than one thousand employees and moved into a new studio in Burbank, California. The studio complex was beautiful and seemed like a small city.

Disney with a collection of his characters

27

WAR AND CHANGE

Technicians working in the recording studio to create the sounds of *Fantasia*

Disney discussing a film production with one of the soldiers in his studio

During World War II (1939–1945), Disney produced more full-length movies, including *Pinocchio, Fantasia, Bambi,* and *Dumbo.* These films cost a great deal of money and took a long time to create. They were supposed to be shown in Europe, but the war prevented this. (Europe was at war years before the United States entered the conflict in late 1941.) Before long, the studio was in financial trouble.

Soon Walt Disney had to face employee trouble too. Many of the staff members were asking for more money, seeing the new studio and thinking the company was rolling in profits. The artists felt underpaid and overworked and wanted a union to represent and protect them. Again, Disney was disappointed and felt that his workers were not loyal to him. On May 29, 1941, most of his artists went on **strike** and, after nine weeks, they won. They had a **union** to protect their rights now, but they no longer had Disney's trust.

In late 1941, with the United States now at war too, Disney was informed that the U.S. Army was taking over his studio. More than seven hundred soldiers lived in the studio for seven months. The army's equipment took over the studio's grounds, and army guards stood at the gate.

To make *Bambi*, Disney's animators spent many hours studying real animals.

> ### Nutziland
>
> Disney's 1942 short film entitled "Der Fuehrer's Face" won an Academy Award. In the movie, Donald Duck dreams about life in "Nutziland," a take-off on Nazi Germany. There he has a terrible job in a factory and barely anything to eat. In the end, he throws tomatoes at a picture of Adolf Hitler, the dictator of Nazi Germany. The comedy helped relieve the tension many people felt during World War II.

For a time, Disney put his regular projects on hold, and the studio began making instructional films for the government. Titles included "Air Craft Carrier Signals" and "Basic Map-Reading." Then the Disney characters got into the act too. Donald Duck was featured in "Der Fuehrer's Face," a short film about Nazi Germany, and also starred in a cartoon encouraging U.S. citizens to pay their taxes on time.

MORE FILM PROJECTS

After the war was over, Disney began producing True-Life Adventure Films, the first of which was *Seal Island*. Then, in 1950, the Disney studio released *Treasure Island*, a live-action film that became a huge hit and marked the beginning of live-action projects for Disney. The studio also began working on three animated features: *Alice in Wonderland, Peter Pan,* and *Cinderella*. The future was looking very bright.

CREATING A KINGDOM

CHAPTER 6

Walt Disney often took his daughters to amusement parks on Sunday mornings. As he walked through these parks, he wondered why they were always so dirty and run-down. And he also noticed that while the children were having fun, the adults were restless. These experiences inspired Disney's next project—the creation of an amusement park that would be different from all others. Of course, people made fun of Disney and discouraged

Tivoli Gardens

One of Walt Disney's inspirations for Disneyland was Tivoli Gardens in Copenhagen, Denmark. This park, which opened in 1843, is quite beautiful. Part amusement park and part botanical garden, it has exciting rides as well as a large collection of flowers and other plants. Tivoli also boasts a wide range of restaurants and hosts many concerts each summer. When Disney visited Tivoli Gardens, he knew it was something special.

31

this project, just as they'd discouraged so many of his other ideas. However, he was determined to build the park—even if he had to pay for it himself—so Disney put up all his life savings, including his house. The park would be called Disneyland.

MAKING PLANS

In December 1952, Walt started WED Enterprises, the company that would create Disneyland. WED was staffed by **Imagineers**, a talented group of architects, engineers, writers, and artists. Walt was happy and relaxed when

Explaining early sketches for Disneyland

he worked with the Imagineers. WED belonged to him and only him, so he enjoyed the time he spent there.

In the meantime, Disney needed to raise money. Television, which was a fairly new invention in the 1950s, was his answer. Most moviemakers saw television as competition to the movie business, but Disney saw it as a tool to make money.

Disney approached a few TV networks with his ideas. With Roy's help, he finally made a deal with the American Broadcasting Companies (ABC) in 1954: ABC would help pay for the park, and Disney would create television programs for ABC. He named his first program *Disneyland* to help advertise the park.

Disneyland on opening day in 1955

DISNEYLAND IS BORN

Meanwhile, Disney had hired a research team who selected 180 acres (73 ha) of land in Orange County, California, as a home for the park. While Disneyland was being built, Disney squatted down everywhere in the park at the height of a child, to make sure a child would feel comfortable anywhere in Disneyland.

33

On July 17, 1955, the park was scheduled to open, but it was not ready. Even the paint was still wet. The park opening was by invitation only, but many people got in with fake invitations, so Disneyland was soon overloaded. There wasn't enough food, and there weren't enough water fountains or even trashcans. The rides broke down, the lines were too long, and the park became covered with litter. The newspapers called the opening "Black Sunday," but Disney used the criticism as an opportunity to prove himself.

Disney spent time in the park looking for every problem he could find. Six months later, as the millionth visitor walked through the gates, Disneyland was truly an extraordinary park. Since then, an average of 23 million people visit the park each year. Guests have included royalty, heads of states, celebrities, and people from all over the world. Disneyland was so successful that Walt and Roy Disney paid off all their debts and became very wealthy. Once again, Walt Disney followed his dream all the way.

opposite: Disney with one of his grandsons at Disneyland

THE MICKEY MOUSE CLUB

Walt Disney was then ready for his next project. On October 3, 1955, he introduced a new children's television program called *The Mickey Mouse Club*. The television show combined singing and dancing with cartoons and live-action film. He chose twenty-four kids to be Mouseketeers, and the public soon knew them all by name. The Mouseketeers loved Uncle Walt, as they called him, and Mickey Mouse ears, like those the Mouseketeers wore, sold at a rate of twenty-four thousand a day.

Eight of the Mouseketeers taking a break for school at the Disney studio

35

Lady and the Tramp premiered in 1955 and was a huge hit.

ON THE BIG SCREEN

Back at the studio, Disney movies experienced both failure and success. Full-length features such as *Lady and the Tramp* and *101 Dalmatians* were huge hits, while *Kidnapped* and *Babes in Toyland* were disappointments.

Disney's next project was making a film of *Mary Poppins,* a story about a magical British governess based on a series of books by P. L. Travers. The final product was filled with live-action actors, animated characters, and special effects. The film, starring Julie Andrews and Dick Van Dyke, premiered in August 1964. *Mary Poppins* received thirteen Academy Award nominations and won five Oscars, including a best actress award for Andrews. The film is now considered a classic.

Julie Andrews in *Mary Poppins*

BRANCHING OUT

Still, with all this success, Disney became restless and began looking for more projects. In 1965 he bought 30,000 acres (12,150 ha) of land in Orlando, Florida. Here he began building a park named Disney World, something like Disneyland, but much bigger. One of Disney's goals for Disney World was the inclusion of a city of the future. He named it EPCOT— Experimental Prototype Community of Tomorrow. The idea consumed him so completely that he even talked about it in his sleep.

Imagining EPCOT

Walt described his vision of EPCOT this way:

EPCOT will be an experimental prototype community of tomorrow that will take its cue from the new ideas and new technologies that are now emerging from the creative centers of American industry. It will be a community of tomorrow that will never be completed, but will always be introducing and testing and demonstrating new materials and systems.

CHAPTER 7
LEAVING A LEGACY

opposite: The grand opening of Walt Disney World in Orlando, Florida

By the mid-1960s, Walt Disney began to look old and tired. He had severe neck and leg pains as well as a horrible cough. His longtime habit of smoking cigarettes had caught up with him, and in 1966 he was told he had lung cancer. Disney tried to keep his illness a secret, and he continued working as much as he could.

By this time, both his daughters were married, and Disney had seven grandchildren. He enjoyed spending time with his big family, and he kept making plans for EPCOT. However, those plans had to continue without him. On December 15, 1966, Walt Disney died in a California hospital. His body was cremated, and the family held a small private memorial service for him. The world mourned the loss of Walt Disney, and many wondered if the company could survive without him.

Always a Child

People all over the world had kind words to say about Walt Disney when he died. Eric Sevareid, a television journalist, remembered him this way:

Walt Disney seemed to know that while there is very little grown-up in a child, there is a lot of child in every grown-up. To a child, this weary world is brand new; Disney tried to keep it that way for adults.

MAKING THE DREAM COME TRUE

By this time, Roy Disney was in his seventies, but he did his best to put his brother's detailed EPCOT plans into action. On October 1, 1971, Roy spoke at the opening of Walt Disney World, having changed the name from

38

Disney World. He wanted the public to know that the new park had been Walt's dream. Only two months later, Roy himself died. It seemed as though his work was finally done.

In October 1982, EPCOT—the second part of Walt Disney World—was officially opened. Disney's original idea for a city of the future had not proved possible. Instead, EPCOT was made into something like a world's fair. It consists of Future World, a showcase for

When finished, EPCOT resulted in a park that is much like a world's fair.

39

American industry, technology, and imagination, and World Showcase, where the cultures and customs of a number of other countries are displayed in individual pavilions.

ONWARD

Since the death of both Walt and Roy Disney, new generations have been given the job of running Walt Disney Productions. At first Roy E. Disney (Roy's son) and Ron Miller (Walt's son-in-law) controlled the business. The 1970s proved to be a hard time for the Disney studio, but then the company created a new film division called Touchstone. Then in 1983 the Disney

Roy E. Disney

A scene from *The Little Mermaid*

Channel cable-television network came into being.

In the 1980s, leadership of Walt Disney Productions was given to Michael Eisner, a well-known Hollywood producer. Under his guidance, the movie division flourished. In addition to movies for adults, the company began producing animated films again. The first big hit was *The Little Mermaid*. In the years since, audiences have enjoyed many Disney films such as *Beauty and the Beast, The Lion King, Mulan, Toy Story,* and *Tarzan*.

A scene from *Mulan*

Director John Lasseter with characters from *Toy Story*

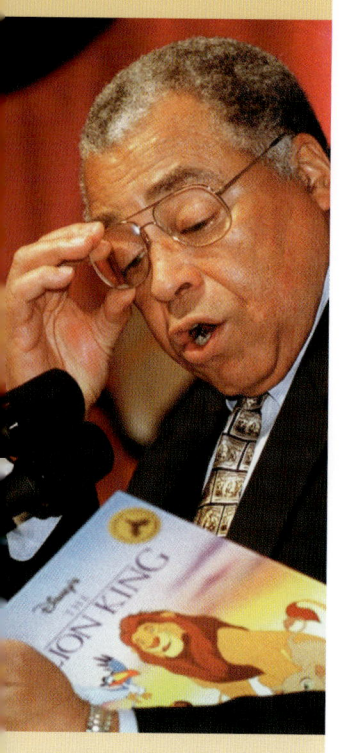

Actor James Earl Jones was the voice of Simba's father, Mufasa, in *The Lion King*.

Alter Ego

It is often true that artists' best creations come from within themselves. Mickey Mouse is no exception. In later years, Walt Disney explained:

The life and ventures of Mickey Mouse have been closely bound up with my own personal and professional life. It is understable that I should have sentimental attachment for the little personage who played so big a part in the course of Disney Productions and has been so happily accepted as an amusing friend wherever films are shown around the world. He still speaks for me and I still speak for him.

A MEMORABLE LIFE

To his credit, Walt Disney never forgot the days when he had nothing. Those days inspired him, and that inspiration led to the creation of Mickey Mouse. It was that unassuming mouse, a mouse who shared his creator's voice, who made Walt Disney's name known and recognized around the world. Mickey Mouse and Walt Disney shared a common goal—to make people smile. They accomplished that goal through cartoons, movies, television shows, amusement parks, and much more. Today, the Walt Disney name stands for an empire, but it all began with a determined man who wanted to entertain his audience.

Fireworks over the Magic Kingdom at Walt Disney World

TIMELINE

1901	Walt Disney is born on December 5 in Chicago, Illinois
1906	Moves with his family to Marceline, Missouri
1910	Moves with his family to Kansas City
1918	Moves with his family back to Chicago; works as an ambulance driver in France at the end of World War I
1919	Gets his first job as an artist
1922	Declares bankruptcy
1923	Moves to Hollywood; goes into business with brother Roy
1925	Marries Lilly Bounds
1927	Creates Oswald the Lucky Rabbit
1928	Creates Mickey Mouse; "Steamboat Willie" premieres
1932	Produces "Flowers and Trees," the first cartoon to use Technicolor
1937	Produces *Snow White and the Seven Dwarfs*
1940	Moves into a new studio
1948	Produces *Seal Island*, the first of the True-Life Adventure Films
1952	Founds WED Enterprises
1954	*Disneyland* premieres on television
1955	Disneyland opens in Anaheim, California; *The Mickey Mouse Club* premieres on television
1964	Produces *Mary Poppins*
1966	Dies on December 15 in California
1971	Walt Disney World opens in Orlando, Florida

GLOSSARY

Academy Awards: the highest honors in film; also called Oscars and presented by the Academy of Motion Picture Arts and Sciences

animation: a motion picture created by filming a series of objects or drawings in different positions; also the process used to create an animated film

animators: artists who creates drawings for an animated film

apprentice: a person who learns a trade or art by working with experienced people

bankruptcy: a state of financial failure or ruin in which personal and business debts cannot be paid

celluloid: a tough material similar to plastic that is used for making films

distributor: a person or company that markets films to theaters

Great Depression: an era in U.S history, marked by unemployment and poverty, that began with the stock-market crash on October 29, 1929

Imagineers: a term used for the creative architects, engineers, writers, and artists at WED Enterprises

live-action films: movies that depict real images of people, animals, and nature—in contrast to animation

multiplane camera: a camera developed to create images with better movement and a three-dimensional feel

strike: a work stoppage by a body of workers, usually with the goal of better working conditions or higher pay

Technicolor: a process that brought full color to film

tuberculosis: a disease affecting the lungs

typhoid fever: an often fatal disease caused by bacteria

union: a group that protects the rights of workers

vaudeville: stage entertainment, often comic, consisting of dancing, singing, acrobats, and performing animals

45

TO FIND OUT MORE

BOOKS

Greene, Katherine, and Richard Greene. *The Man Behind the Magic: The Story of Walt Disney.* New York: Viking Children's Books, 1998.

Hahn, Don. *Disney's Animation Magic: A Behind-the-Scenes Look at How an Animated Film Is Made.* New York: Hyperion, 1996.

Hammontree, Marie, and Fred Irvin (illustrator). *Walt Disney: Young Movie Maker.* New York: Aladdin, 1997.

Nardo, Don. *The Importance of Walt Disney.* Minneapolis: Lerner, 2000.

Schroeder, Russell, and Howard Reeves (editors). *Walt Disney: His Life in Pictures.* New York: Disney Press, 1996.

Schultz, Ron, and Chris Brigmna (illustrator). *Looking Inside Cartoon Animation.* New York: Avalon, 1992.

Selden, Bernice. *The Story of Walt Disney: Maker of Magical Worlds.* New York: Bantam Doubleday Dell Books for Young Readers, 1989.

Simon, Charnan. *Walt Disney: Creator of Magical Worlds.* Danbury, Conn.: Children's Press, 1999.

INTERNET SITES

Academy of Motion Picture Arts and Sciences
http://www.oscars.org/index.html
The official site of the Academy Awards.

Disney.com
http://www.disney.go.com
The official Disney site.

JustDisney.com
http://www.justdisney.com
For biographical information about Walt Disney plus the latest Disney news.

A Tribute to Walt Disney
http://www.waltdisneylife.com/
A tribute to Walt Disney; contains information on his life, photos, and famous quotes as well as a listing of his animated films.

Walt Disney
http://fuv.hivolda.no/prosjekt/gunnargrodal/bio.htm
A biography of Walt Disney.

INDEX

Page numbers in *italics* indicate illustrations.

Academy Awards, 5, 22, 24, 26, *27*, 37
"Air Craft Carrier Signals" instructional film, 30
Alice in Wonderland, 30
Alice's Wonderland cartoon series, 16, 18, 20
American Broadcasting Companies (ABC), 33
Andrews, Julie, 37, *37*
animation, 4, 15, 18, 21
Art Institute of Chicago, 12, *13*

Babes in Toyland, 36
Bambi, 28, *29*
"Basic Map Reading" instructional film, 30
Beauty and the Beast, 41
Bounds, Lillian. *See* Disney, Lillian.
Burbank, California, 27

celluloid, 15
Chaplin, Charlie, 12, *12*
Chicago, Illinois, 7, 12, *13*
Cinderella, 30

"Der Fuehrer's Face" short film, 30
Disney Brothers Studio, 18
Disney, Diane Marie (daughter), 6, 25, *25*, 31
Disney, Elias (father), 7, 8–9, 11, 27
Disney, Flora (mother), 7, 27
Disney, Herbert (brother), 7, 8
Disney, Lillian (wife), 6, 19, *19*, 21, 25, *25*
Disney, Raymond (brother), 7, 8
Disney, Roy (brother), 6, 7, 8, 9, 11, 14, 17, 18, *18*, 19, 27, 35, 38

Disney, Roy E. (nephew), 40, *40*
Disney, Ruth (sister), 7, 8
Disney, Sharon Mae (daughter), 6, 25, *25*, 31
Disney, Walter Elias, *4*, 7, *14*, *16*, *18*, *19*, *23*, *24*, *25*, *26*, *27*, *28*, *32*, *34*, *42*
  artistic talent of, 8, 12, 13
  birth of, 7
  childhood of, 7–8, 9, 11
  death of, 38
  marriage of, 19
Disneyland, 4, 32–35, *32*, *33*, *34*. *See also* EPCOT; Walt Disney World.
Disneyland television program, 33
Donald Duck, 4, 27, 30
Dumbo, 28

Eisner, Michael, 41
EPCOT (Experimental Prototype Community of Tomorrow), 37, 38, 39–40, *39*. *See also* Disneyland; Walt Disney World.

Fantasia, 28, *28*
films. *See* individual titles.
"Flowers and Trees" cartoon, 24
Future World, 39–40

Goofy, 4, 27
government films, 30
Great Depression, 24

Hollywood, California, 17–18, *17*

Imagineers, 32–33
Iwerks, Ub, 14, 15, 16, *16*, 19, 21, 24
Iwerks-Disney studio, 15, 17

The Jazz Singer (film), 19, 22, *22*
Jolson, Al, 22, *22*
Jones, James Earl, *42*

Kansas City Film Ad Company, 15, 16
Kansas City, Missouri, 9, *9*, 14
Kidnapped, 36

Lady and the Tramp, 36, *36*
Lasseter, John, *41*
Laugh-O-Gram Films, 16, 17
Laugh-O-Grams, 15–16
The Lion King, 41
The Little Mermaid, 40, 41
"Little Tramp." *See* Chaplin, Charlie.

Marceline, Missouri, 7, 8
Mary Poppins, 36–37, *37*
Mickey Mouse, 4, *5*, 21, 22, *23*, 24, *42*, 43
The Mickey Mouse Club television program, 35, *35*
Mickey Mouse ears, 35
Miller, Ron, 40
Minnie Mouse, *5*
Mintz, Charles, 20
Mouseketeers, 35, *35*
movies. *See* individual titles.
Mulan, 41, *41*
multiplane cameras, 25

101 Dalmations, 36
Oscar awards. *See* Academy Awards.
Oswald the Lucky Rabbit, 20

Pesmen-Rubin Commercial Art Studio, 14

47

INDEX (continued)

Peter Pan, 30
Pinocchio, 28
Pluto, 27
Presidential Medal of Freedom, 5

Red Cross Ambulance Unit, 13, *13*

Seal Island, 30
Sevareid, Eric, 38
silent movies, 12, 19
Silly Symphonies, 24
Snow White and the Seven Dwarfs, 25–26, *26*
"Steamboat Willie" cartoon short, 22

"Talkies," 22
Tarzan, 41
Technicolor, 24
television, 33
Temple, Shirley, *27*
"The Tiny Voice" cartoon strip, 13
Tivoli Gardens, 31, *31*
Touchstone Pictures, 40
Toy Story, 41, *41*
Travers, P. L., 36
Treasure Island, 30
True-Life Adventure Films, 30

Universal Pictures, 20, 21–22

Van Dyke, Dick, 37

Walt Disney Studios, 18, 20, 21, 24, 27, 29, *35*, 40, 41
Walt Disney World, 4, 37, 38, *39*, 43. See also Disneyland; EPCOT.
WED Enterprises, 32, 33
Winkler, Margaret, 18, 20
World War I, 13
World War II, 28, 29, 30

About the Author

Elizabeth Dana Jaffe received her undergraduate degree from Brown University and went on to earn a master's degree in early education from Bankstreet College in New York City. She has edited various educational materials for children and has written numerous books, including a biography of Sojourner Truth, a book about pilots, a series of books about games, and *Can You Eat a Fraction?* She lives in New York City.